THIS CANDLEWICK BOOK BELONGS TO:

_____

_____

_____

For Caz, Beth, and Alice, who saw it through
M. J.

Text copyright © 2014 by Martin Jenkins
Illustrations copyright © 2014 by Satoshi Kitamura

First U.S. paperback edition 2015

Library of Congress Catalog Card Number 2013952840

ISBN 978-0-7636-6763-4 (hardcover)
ISBN 978-0-7636-7973-6 (paperback)

15 16 17 18 19 20 CCP 10 9 8 7 6 5 4 3 2 1

Printed in Shenzhen, Guangdong, China

This book was typeset in Triplex Serif.
The illustrations were done in watercolor.

Candlewick Press
99 Dover Street
Somerville, Massachusetts 02144

visit us at www.candlewick.com

The HISTORY of MONEY

FROM BARTERING TO BANKING

Martin Jenkins

ILLUSTRATED BY
Satoshi Kitamura

CANDLEWICK PRESS

— Contents —

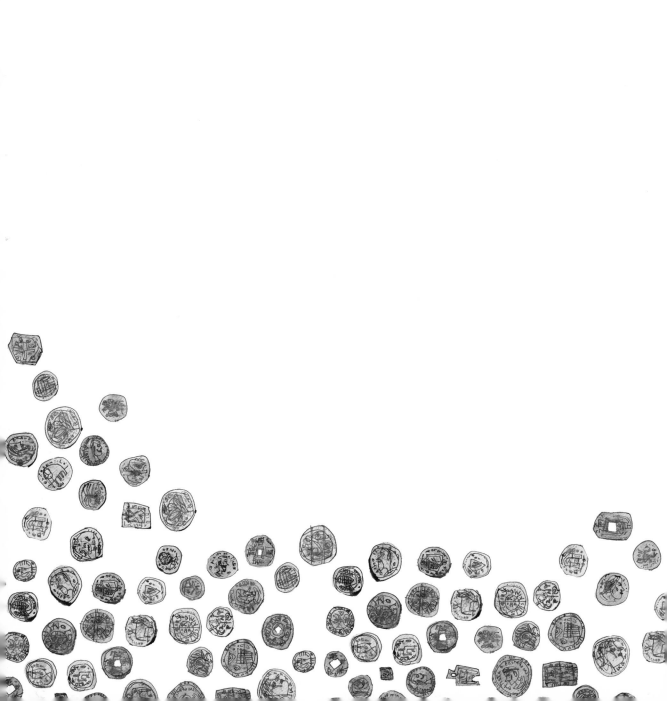

— Introduction —

IN the Yap Islands in the South Pacific, it can be a huge stone with a hole in the middle. In Sweden 350 years ago, it was great copper slabs that you needed a donkey to carry. It can be a string of shells or a bundle of special cloth. Nowadays it's likely to be a row of ones and zeroes in a computer somewhere. Some people have tons of it—more than most of us could possibly imagine. An awful lot of people have none at all, or so little that it makes no difference. We all know where it goes, but it's really hard to figure out where it comes from. Some people think it's the most wonderful thing; others think it's really, really bad. But we all seem to agree that one way or another, it's pretty important.

So what is it?

It's money, of course. The stuff that makes the world go around. That doesn't grow on trees. That can't buy you love, apparently.

Once upon a time there wasn't any. And it's safe to assume that people then got along fine without it, just as some people in some parts of the world manage perfectly well without it today. So why would anyone have gone to the trouble of inventing it? And when?

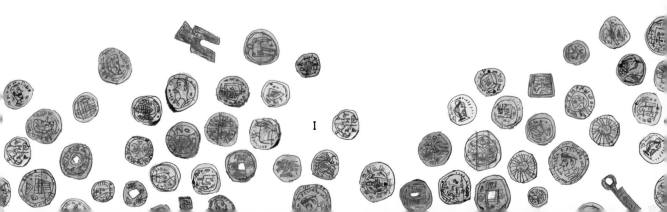

I

— Chapter One —
In which nobody has any money

WE know from archaeology that for a long, long time, humans have had tools, clothes, and ornaments, and we can be sure that they had these things long before they had money, or any need for money.

We think that very early in human history, people lived in family groups, hunting and gathering food and moving from place to place. The things they used would have been made from materials that they could get hold of quite easily: tools from stones and bits of bone, clothes from animal skins or bark. If anyone needed anything, they were usually able to make it themselves or borrow it from someone else in the group. It's possible that the head of the group decided who needed what and when and handed things around accordingly.

At some point, things changed. It might have gone something like this. Suppose you were living in one of those groups, and you found you were especially good at something useful—making javelins out of yew wood, perhaps. Soon everyone in the group would want one of your special yew-wood javelins. At first you might just give them away—after all, what was yours was everyone's, in your group at least, and you'd be rather proud of the fact that you could make better javelins than anyone else's. But perhaps you'd find that you were so busy making them that you didn't have enough time to go out and collect your own food. So people in your group would start to give you food in return for a new javelin.

It might not just be objects, such as javelins, that people could offer others. One person might be able to use herbs to cure people when they were sick; another might be an expert at setting broken bones. People would ask for their help when they needed their skills and give them something in return.

Your group might also get in the habit of exchanging things with other groups. Some of this exchanging would have been a way of showing friendship—the way we give presents to people today. And some of it may have been because it was useful for both groups: you might have some extra wolf-fur cloaks that you could swap for a load of dried fish from a group that

3

had had a good fishing season—both really useful things for getting through the winter. That would be the start of what we call barter: swapping something you have that another person wants for something they have that you want.

That being said, we don't actually know for sure that barter was an important part of people's lives tens of thousands of years ago. Possibly not—after all, people always moving from place to place wouldn't have needed or wanted much stuff—one good fur cloak and perhaps a couple of javelins would do you nicely. Why would you carry more than that around with you?

— Chapter Two —
In which nobody has any money
but people do have lots of stuff

BUT then, around the end of the last Ice Age, people started to do something that would change the world forever. Instead of moving around and gathering wild plants and hunting animals, they began to grow plants and keep animals. Strangely, they seem to have started doing this in different parts of the world at roughly the same time. But as far as we know, the first place it happened, more than 11,000 years ago, was in the Middle East, in a region known as the Fertile Crescent. And it's here that the story of money really takes off.

Once people started growing plants in fields, they started staying in the same place for long stretches of time, perhaps permanently. And once they were living in one place, they could begin to collect stuff—lots of stuff. And we can be sure they would start caring about who owned what. This new way of doing things was quite hard work—clearing land, tilling it, sowing seeds, looking after the growing plants, and harvesting the crop; or finding good pasture for your flocks, protecting them from wild animals, and keeping them sheltered during the winter. You wouldn't want to do all that and then have someone else come along and help themselves to the best parts of your crop or your finest young lambs.

Rather than a single person owning land or flocks of sheep, it was probably families or whole clans, who would have a way of sharing things among themselves. As time went on, the clans who had gotten hold of the best parcels of land would be able to harvest more crops or breed more sheep and goats than they needed to get through to the next harvest. These clans would be in a good position to barter for other things. It might be horses, or clothes, or furniture—now that they were living in one place they might well have a house to live in and furnish. Or they might swap a lamb or two for some help in building a new grain store, or for a slave, or for another wife for the head of the clan.

— Chapter Three —
In which we start counting the things that count

WE know that some goods were carried long distances in the Fertile Crescent because things like shells have been found in ancient settlements a long way from where they are found in nature. We can't be certain, but we're pretty sure that these shells were traded. And there's another really good clue that trade of some sort was taking place. Around 10,000 years ago, people began to make lots of little objects out of clay, mostly simple shapes like balls or cones, but also tiny models of animals and tools. These shapes often had small holes in them, as if they were meant to be strung together. We think these objects were a way of keeping track of things that you owned.

Sometimes many objects of one kind were sealed inside a clay envelope. This might record how many sacks of wheat you had in a village grain store, for example. You would hand over the grain and get an envelope with that

7

number of tokens in it, so that you could open the envelope and get the right amount of grain back when you needed it. Or perhaps you could get other goods that were worth the same amount as the grain you had in the store.

These clay envelopes were used for thousands of years. At some point people must have realized that if you could see from the outside how many tokens there were inside, then you wouldn't have to smash the clay envelope every time you needed to count them.

Using the blunt end of a reed, they pressed simple pictures into the clay on the outside of the envelope before it had dried: ten tokens inside and you'd press ten circles onto the outside. Later still, they worked out that if you had a drawing of the number of tokens, then you didn't really need the tokens at all. So instead of big clay envelopes, they started keeping records on clay tablets. At roughly the same time, they began using a kind of shorthand. Instead of drawing, say, 100 tiny sheep symbols on one tablet, they drew one sheep symbol and next to it a sign meaning "a hundred" and then a sign indicating who owned the hundred sheep. From there, it wasn't very far to real writing. But that's for another chapter.

— Chapter Four —
In which we discuss goat swapping

BARTERING is very useful, but there's a problem with it: you can only swap something you've already got for something you need or want. Suppose you're a goat farmer and you need some grain for the winter. You might offer a grain farmer a goat in return for two sacks of wheat.

But the grain farmer might not want any goats: he might have nowhere to keep them, or he might have enough goats of his own. Of course he could take your goats and try to swap them with somebody else for something he did want, but he'd have to find someone who wanted goats and had things he wanted, and he'd have to look after the goats in the meantime.

Wouldn't it be handy if you could swap your goat for something easy to keep and carry around and that everybody wanted? Then you could find someone who had some of this something and wanted a goat. You'd trade one of your goats for the stuff and then go to the grain farmer and swap the

stuff for some grain. The grain farmer would then have the stuff which he in turn could trade with someone else for something he wanted. Everyone would end up with what he or she wanted. Brilliant.

It would be even better if the stuff was easy to divide into different amounts. Say you had one goat to spare but only wanted half a goat's worth of grain. If you wanted the goat to stay alive, you couldn't very well hand over half of it. Now you could swap your goat for half a goat's worth of grain *and* half a goat's worth of stuff, and then keep the stuff to swap for something else.

The question was: What could this stuff be?

— Chapter Five —
In which we get on to the hard stuff

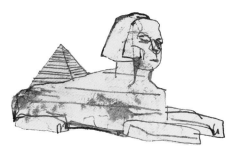

AT the same time that people were growing wheat and domesticating sheep and inventing writing, they began doing something else that might have seemed strange. They were picking up lumps of metal. There was iron from meteorites—that was extremely rare. And greeny-red copper—there was a fair bit of that if you knew where to look. There were also whitish or yellow nuggets. The really yellow ones were heavy and very rare, but the whitish or whitish-yellow ones were more common and not so heavy. The yellow nuggets were gold, the whitish ones silver, and the in-between ones were a mixture of gold and silver called electrum.

These metals were fascinating. Gold especially was amazing. It kept its beautiful shiny color no matter what you did with it—it never seemed to stain or rot, and it didn't burn. By beating and rolling a nugget, you could turn it into pretty much any shape, and if you heated it in a fire, you could draw it out into a thread. Silver and copper were almost as magical. They went dull quite quickly but could soon be polished up again. They weren't quite as easy to shape, and if you beat them a lot, they might start to split or fall apart, but heating them generally solved that.

You couldn't make anything very big out of the metals, as the nuggets

were almost always small and nobody had yet worked out how to combine the metal from separate nuggets. In any case, they were too rare, and, in the case of gold and silver, too soft to be of much use in making tools or weapons — certainly not as useful as much commoner stuff, like flint or bone. But they could be made into beautiful ornaments and pieces of jewelry, like amulets or bracelets.

As time went on, people found ways of extracting big amounts of some metals — especially copper, tin, and iron — from rocks and, by using really hot fires, of making tools and weapons out of them. These metals began to play an important practical part in everyday life, but gold, silver, and electrum remained special. We can be sure that most gold

ended up in the hands of powerful people like priests and rulers, although we can't tell, in the age before writing, whether it was traded or whether they just took it.

We do know, though, that silver and electrum were traded, especially silver. In fact, by the time writing came along, they had become a really important part of trade—they'd become that "stuff" that you could swap for pretty much anything. They had become money.

— Chapter Six —
In which we find out how expensive
it is to bite a man's nose

WHEN silver started to be used as money, it was the weight that mattered, not the number of pieces. Some of the earliest writing we can understand is all about the price of things in weight of silver. Not just stuff like timber and cattle, but daily wages and fines. According to the law code of the king of Eshnunna in Mesopotamia (part of the Fertile Crescent) around 4,000 years ago, the fine for biting a man's nose was one mina of silver. That's about one pound — quite a lot. A slap in the face cost 10 shekels, or one-sixth of a mina. The daily wage of someone harvesting barley was just 12 se, or a thousandth of a mina. So if you bit someone's nose, you'd have had to work every day for nearly three years to pay off the fine.

BITING A NOSE · I POUND OF SILVER (I MINA)

Even a tiny amount of silver money, like 12 se — just a fifth of an ounce or so — was clearly a lot for some people. It was a day's wages, after all, so it was very important that whoever dealt with money had a good pair of scales and some accurate weights, and a way of telling that the stuff that was traded really was silver (though we still don't really understand how they knew that). It seems that in Mesopotamia and, later, in ancient Egypt, it was the temples that were in charge. If you wanted to buy or sell something using silver, you probably had to go to the temple to do it.

The priests in the temples kept the weights and recorded who had bought and sold what, but it was the rulers who made the laws and regulations about money. As well as fixing the amount for fines and taxes, they decided the prices for different things, such as oil or cloth. Most things were valued in silver, but not everything. Barley was also used as a kind of money for food, even though its value would change from year to year depending on how good the harvest was. People in other places also began using metal and grain as kinds of money. The metal wasn't always silver: in Egypt it was mainly copper, along with some gold, as silver was very rare.

— Chapter Seven —
Which we think will be of interest

EVEN in places like Mesopotamia and ancient Egypt, where money was important, lots of people would have had very little or none most of the time. If you were one of them, you would have bartered for the things you needed, and if you had nothing to barter, you would have borrowed. You might have run out of food before the harvest was ready, and had to borrow some from someone else, promising to repay them at harvesttime. Or you might want to borrow someone's cattle to plow your fields, and again promise to pay them back with some of your crop at harvest time. Borrowing would only work if the person lending was sure that you'd stay around long enough to be able to repay them, and if they were pretty sure that you could repay them — that

GOOD HARVEST

THANKS A LOT, HERE ARE THE 2 BAGS I OWE YOU.

your harvest would be good enough to feed your family with enough extra to pay them back.

Exactly how much you should repay is something people have been arguing about throughout history and are still arguing about today. A lot of people say that if someone lends you three sacks of barley, then you should repay three sacks of barley. That seems fair. But it doesn't take into account the fact that it's a bit risky lending things to people: their harvest might fail, or they might leave, or even die, before they could repay you. Some people argue that because of all this, you should pay someone back a bit more than you originally borrowed. They would also say that if someone lent you a sack of barley for seed at planting time, and you harvested twenty sacks of barley at the end of the season, you should pay back the original sack plus a portion of the nineteen extra sacks. After all, without the original seed, you wouldn't have managed to harvest any barley at all.

There's another reason why people can get more back than they lend. The thing they're lending is often more important to the person borrowing than it is to them. Whatever it is, the lender is likely to have more than they need, otherwise they wouldn't be too eager to lend it. If they

BAD HARVEST

had a big crop of barley one year, with a lot to spare, they'd hardly miss a few sacks for someone else. But for that other person, or their family, if their own crop had failed, it might be literally a matter of life or death. That means the person lending is in a position to drive a hard bargain. It doesn't seem quite fair, does it? But it's the way an awful lot of business has been carried out since business first started being carried out.

The amount extra you usually have to pay back when you borrow is called the interest. The king of Eshnunna's code says that if you borrow silver, to buy an ox, for example, then at the end of the year you have to pay back a fifth as much silver again as you originally borrowed. That's an interest rate of 20 percent.

— Chapter Eight —
In which we discover that money is the root of all writing

BORROWING must have been hard to arrange before the invention of writing. People's memories often play tricks on them, and it would have been very easy for someone to "forget" after six months or a year exactly how much they'd borrowed, or even if they'd borrowed anything at all. You could have other people there as witnesses, but there would be arguments if some people remembered one amount and some

another. But if you scratched the details into a clay tablet, which you baked in a fire so that you couldn't change it afterward, you'd have a record that it would be much harder to argue about.

These tablets are what we call IOUs ("I owe you"—simple isn't it?).

 = **I Owe You**

Sometimes an IOU named the person who owed something and the person who was owed. "I, Amil-mirra, owe Josephat thirty pieces of silver, which I will repay on the first full moon after New Year." That kind of thing.

The IOU would be kept by the person who was owed or in a safe place like a temple. On the due date, if everything went according to plan, the thirty pieces of silver would be handed over and the IOU would be destroyed, and that would be that.

I, AMIL-MIRRA, OWE JOSEPHAT THIRTY PIECES OF SILVER, WHICH I WILL REPAY ON THE FIRST FULL MOON AFTER NEW YEAR.

AMIL-MIRRA

JOSEPHAT

The only person who could use this kind of IOU would be the person named on it as owed money. That means that if Josephat owed Iris thirty pieces of silver, this would have to be recorded in a separate IOU. Iris would have to wait until Amil-mirra had paid Josephat on the due date to get her silver from Josephat. The second IOU would be destroyed in turn.

I, JOSEPHAT, OWE IRIS THIRTY PIECES OF SILVER, WHICH I WILL REPAY ON THE SECOND FULL MOON AFTER NEW YEAR.

JOSEPHAT

IRIS

But sometimes IOUs just named the person who owed the money. "I, Amil-mirra, will pay the person who has this tablet thirty pieces of silver . . ." In lots of ways this kind of IOU is more useful. Amil-mirra would hand it over to Josephat and then when Josephat owed Iris, instead of writing out a new IOU, he could simply hand over the original one to Iris, leaving her to collect the silver directly from Amil-mirra. If Iris ended up owing someone else, she could hand over the IOU in her turn.

AMIL-MIRRA   JOSEPHAT   IRIS

Archaeologists have found lots and lots of tablets from ancient Mesopotamia of this sort. They're as important in the history of money as the discovery of precious metals—and they may well be the main reason writing was invented in the first place.

— Chapter Nine —
In which we start coining it

WITH weights of metal—called bullion—and grain used as ways of measuring money, and with clay tablets as IOUs and for keeping track of who owned what, everything seems to have gone on perfectly well. Then, around 600 BCE, another great idea came along: the coin. A coin was a piece of metal of a particular size and shape, usually with something on it to tell you how much it weighed and a sign or symbol to show you where it was produced or minted, often a portrait of the ruler. Like lots of ancient inventions, coins seem to have appeared in different parts of the world at roughly the same time, popping up in China and around the Black Sea, as well as in the eastern parts of the Mediterranean region, where there were hundreds of mini-countries, or city-states, each with its own rulers and laws.

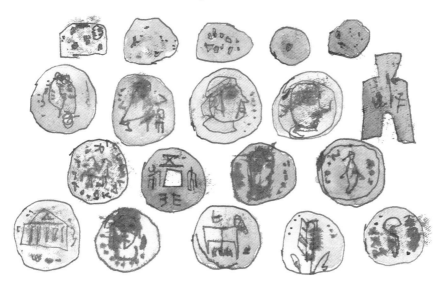

The most obvious reason to have coins is that if you know how much each one weighs, and therefore how much it's worth, you don't have to weigh it every time you want to use it. So you don't have to go off to the temple every time you want to buy or sell something. This makes it much easier to do business. It's probably no coincidence that one of the first places to use

coins—Lydia, in what is now Turkey—was, according to the ancient Greek writer Herodotus, the first place to have actual shops.

At first, coins in Lydia and other places in the Mediterranean were made of valuable metals like gold, silver, or electrum. They would have been useful for rich people trading expensive goods or as a handy way of saving, but they wouldn't have been much good for buying day-to-day things like food. Eventually much less valuable coins made of copper or bronze were produced for everyday use. Thousands have been found at the sites of ancient markets in places like Athens, in Greece, showing how often they were used.

For a long time not all city-states made their own coins, but those that did often insisted that only their money be used when buying and selling in their city. The coins had a value that was a bit higher than the actual value of the metal in them, which meant that the rulers of the states could make a profit from minting them. This was the beginning of what we call currency. Money changers sprang up, greeting merchants at ports and border crossings and exchanging their bullion or foreign coins for local currency, also making a tidy profit at the same time. Some of these money changers were really the first bankers we know about. As well as changing money, they looked after it for other people and lent it out—at a good rate of interest, of course.

The most famous early banker was named Pasion. He lived at Piraeus, the port town of Athens, and started out as a slave, helping his masters, who owned a bank. He was so good at business that he eventually took over the bank and was even made a free man and citizen of Athens, something very unusual for slaves in those days. When he died, in 370 BCE, he was said to have been worth more than 360,000 drachmas, an enormous fortune, showing how profitable banking could be even then.

— Chapter Ten —
Which might be a little bit taxing

THE people who deposited their money with bankers like Pasion were often travelers who had nowhere safe to keep it. But sometimes they were people trying to hide their money from tax collectors—since if there's one thing that we can be pretty sure is as old as money, it's taxes.

Rulers and governments have always wanted money for all sorts of things. It might be for the general good of their country and its citizens—to build roads, or run schools, or defend the country from other people. Or it might be so that the rulers can live in the style to which they're accustomed or build grand monuments to themselves, like the Egyptian pyramids. Whatever the reasons, rulers have been pretty inventive about how they've gone about raising money. The king of Eshnunna's fines for nose biting and other things was one way, and the fee from minting coins was another. Conquering foreign lands and taking their riches has often been popular—although the problem with that is you need funds to raise and equip an army before you can set about conquering and plundering.

But the most common way to raise money has always been through taxation, where rulers or governments take a proportion of the amount that people own, earn, or spend. In the past, it was common for people who had no money, or very little of it, to pay their taxes in kind. That is, they would give their rulers a portion of the food they grew, for example, or work for them without pay for a part of the year. On the whole, though, rulers have preferred to get their taxes in money. And, of course for as long there have been taxes, people have been trying to find ways to avoid paying them.

— Chapter Eleven —
In which the Romans inflate

FOR at least two hundred years after coins were in everyday use in most of the Greek world, the Romans and their neighbors the Etruscans were still using bronze bullion as money. It wasn't very convenient—bronze wasn't that valuable, so you needed a lot of it to make up any big amount. It's said that Roman senators of the time had to carry their wealth around in carts (driven or hauled by slaves, of course).

Around 200 BCE, the Romans finally started using coins made of silver and bronze. The main ones were the bronze as and the silver denarius, which was originally worth 10 asses.

At about this time, they also started trying to take over the rest of the world. Money from kingdoms they defeated poured into Rome, in the form of booty, tributes, and taxes. When the kingdom of Macedon fell in 167 BCE, 75 million denarii—more than 300 tons of silver—is said to have come to Rome. Of course, it was Rome's rulers who actually got their hands on most of it—a very good reason to become a politician.

As Rome became more powerful, the number of people in the city increased, and so did the money they spent. A lot of it went to luxuries—extravagant banquets, spectacular games and circuses, exotic animals, fancy furniture, clothing, and perfumes and spices imported from Arabia, China, and India. The Roman historian Pliny wrote that in the first century CE, more than 25 million denarii a year was spent importing luxury goods from the East. All this money, in the form of silver and gold, left Rome.

The growing population in Rome meant that more and more people needed money to buy and sell things. As long as the empire grew, silver and gold coins and metals kept coming in from the conquered lands, and so there was generally enough to keep people happy. But after around 117 CE, the empire stopped growing and there were few new sources of precious metals. Coins were still leaving the city in large amounts to pay for imports, and there began to be a shortage in Rome itself.

The city's rulers thought they could solve the problem by mixing the silver that went into denarii and other high-value coins with common metals, what we call base metals, such as lead and tin. That way each given amount of silver would make more denarii, and there would be more money to go around.

But the merchants knew perfectly well what was happening and simply raised their prices, so that they still got the same weight of silver as before. As prices went up, eventually people were forced to pay higher wages as well. A legionary soldier, who was paid 225 denarii a year in Julius Caesar's time (about 46 BCE), was paid 600 denarii a year 250 years later, in 200 CE, and 1,800 denarii a year in 235 CE. But the denarii in Julius Caesar's time were almost entirely silver, while those in 235 CE were less than one part in ten silver and you needed far more of them to buy the same amount of food or clothing. By playing around in this way with their coinage, the Romans had invented what we now call inflation.

— Chapter Twelve —
In which we discover the real cost of precious metals

WHEN Christopher Columbus sailed west into the Atlantic in 1492, he was trying to find a way around the world to eastern Asia, but he was also looking for gold. He didn't find Asia; he found a new world—America—instead. He also found gold, on the island of Hispaniola, in the Caribbean. It was enough to make him rich, but the amount he found was tiny compared with the vast amounts discovered in Central and South America by the Spanish conquistadors who followed him. Native peoples, including the Aztecs in Mexico and the Incas in Peru, used gold and silver not as money but to make ornaments and jewelry. What the Spaniards found they took and melted down, to ship as bullion back to Spain to be turned into coins.

They soon discovered the source of the metals, too, most famously at Potosí in Bolivia, the site of the biggest silver mine the world has ever seen. Between 1556 and 1783, 45,000 tons of silver were dug out of the mine by local people forced to work in the most terrible conditions. Thousands of miners died from accidents and exhaustion and from poisoning by the mercury that was used in the mining. When there were no longer enough native people left to work the mines, the Spaniards imported slaves from Africa, who died in huge numbers in their turn.

The silver and gold from mines like Potosí made Spain a rich country for a while. But it doesn't seem to have done the Spanish people much good in

the long run. The Spaniards didn't come up with new ways of doing business or making things or growing food, although the money did pay for a few wars. Its main effect seems to have been to make things more expensive—in other words, it caused inflation. This meant that poor people—that is, most people—could afford to buy even less than before. It's strange that sometimes, as in the time of the Roman Empire, a shortage of precious metal led to inflation, while at other times, as in Spain in the seventeenth century, having a lot of it had the same effect.

— Chapter Thirteen —
Which includes an interesting fact about gold

PEOPLE all over the world still buy things with coins, but the ones that we use from day to day are never made out of precious metal, and haven't been for over a hundred years. One good reason is that, as in ancient Rome, there simply isn't enough to go around. After thousands of years of effort, and countless lives lost, the amount of gold we humans have succeeded in digging out of the ground would fill a cube just 65 feet by 65 feet by 65 feet (20 meters by 20 meters by 20 meters). That's only a little more than a cubic centimeter, or 23 grams, for each person in the world. Some of this is in the form of jewelry, but an awful lot is in bars, locked away in bank vaults. Amazing, isn't it, going to all that trouble to dig the stuff out of one hole just to put it away in another?

In fact, the money that we use now, and that economists, politicians, and bankers talk about all the time, has very little to do with precious metals. Instead, it's really various sorts of IOUs. The idea of these has been around for an awfully long time. Remember those Sumerian clay tablets? They acted as a sort of currency, but one with quite limited use. Generally they named the person who owed money and the date the money was due to be paid. The IOU would only be used by someone who actually knew the person named on it and trusted him or her to pay the money when it was due. But when big powerful organizations like governments or banks get involved, then the IOUs can be much more widely used. And that's just what happened.

— Chapter Fourteen —
In which coins go out (for a while) and paper comes in

THE first place to introduce paper money was China, around 1000 CE. At that time, copper coins were the most common form of money, but, as trade within China grew and coins left the country to pay for imported goods, there was a shortage, as had happened with silver in Rome nearly a thousand years earlier. To try to stop this, the emperor banned people from paying for things directly with copper coins. Instead they were supposed to exchange their coins for paper bills issued by the government. Each bill stated how much it was worth in metal coins, and people were to use them in the same way as coins. Every few years, they would have to swap their bills for a new set produced by the government printers. They wouldn't get quite as many back as they handed in, so the government made a nice little profit in the process. Lots of people didn't totally trust the paper money and broke the rules by bartering or paying with coins on the quiet. Still, the system lasted a couple of hundred years before it was finally abandoned.

In China, paper money came about by

a decree from the all-powerful emperor, but in Europe, it was banks that led the way. Modern banking really began in Italy in around the twelfth century. Families such as the Medicis in Florence became extremely rich and

powerful by dealing in money. Like Pasion in Athens 1,500 years earlier, they exchanged currencies, took deposits from people, and lent out money, charging a healthy fee for doing so. They also bought and sold the credit notes—or IOUs—of merchants, also charging a fee each time. It wasn't just ordinary people who used the banks owned by these great families. They were also used by rulers and governments, who always needed money for their grand plans, which often involved waging war with other states.

Eventually, European governments began to issue paper money themselves, as the Chinese emperor had done hundreds of years before. The first country to do this was Sweden, in 1661, but it only lasted there for just over ten years. Then, in 1694, the Bank of England was founded in London and began to issue sterling banknotes, which it still does. Other countries copied the idea and, with many hiccups, we gradually arrived at the system

we have today, with most countries in the world having their own currency and issuing banknotes and nonprecious metal coins in that currency.

Sometimes a group of countries decides to use the same currency. In Africa, fourteen different countries use one called the CFA franc, created in 1945, and in Europe most countries now use the euro, which was created in 1999. Sharing a currency can make life easier in a lot of ways—it's much simpler for people in different countries to trade with one another, for example—but it seems to create quite a lot of other problems in the long run. This has been happening in Europe since 2008, when there was a big financial crisis that is still causing challenges and problems.

— Chapter Fifteen —
In which we discover how easy it is
for money to disappear

PERHAPS in the end the most important fact about money—and the hardest thing to understand about it—is that it exists only because people believe in it. It's not a physical thing—even though that's how we tend to think of it, as banknotes and coins, or cash.

In fact if you take all the banknotes and coins that are being used at one time in a country and add them all up, the total amount will be much less than the amount of money that people believe exists at that time. A huge amount is on deposit in bank accounts. Normally that's fine, since these days we use cash less and less when we're buying and selling things (instead, we use bank cards and all sorts of electronic banking, and more old-fashioned things like checks). But if a lot of people were to decide at the same time that they wanted to have all their money in cash, then there could be a problem. There isn't nearly enough to go around.

It's not just that there isn't enough cash around to cover the money that people think they have in the bank; it's that the banks don't really have the money at all. The way banks work, as they always have, is that they are given money by people to look after, which they then lend to other people to do things like buy houses. The banks charge interest on the money they've lent out. Sometimes they pay interest to the people who have deposited money with them, but they always pay less interest than they charge, and that's one of the main ways they make a profit.

In most countries, the banks aren't allowed to lend out all the money that people have deposited with them. They have to keep some as cash in their vaults and, usually, some as deposits with the central bank of the country. This is normally around one-twentieth of the amount that people have given to them to look after. Mostly that doesn't matter because only a tiny proportion of the money people have deposited in the bank is taken out in any one day and the bank has enough to cover it. But if a lot of people started to worry—because they thought the bank had lent their money to people (or governments) who might not pay it back—then they might all try to take their money out at once. And then there'd be a real problem, since the bank simply wouldn't be able to pay them. Even if it could get back most or all of what it had lent out, it couldn't do it quickly enough to hand over the money to the people wanting it. The bank would stop working, and if the government didn't step in, the people who had money deposited with the bank would lose all or almost all of it. It would just disappear, as if it had never existed. This is called a run on the bank, and it happens quite often—certainly more often than most bankers would like to admit.

— Chapter Sixteen —
In which we discover that even when money doesn't disappear, you still can't pin it down

WE think of money as a physical thing, and we tend to think it has a fixed value. Neither of these is true. The amount you can buy with, say, one U.S. dollar or one British pound is always changing. Usually as time goes on, you can buy less and less with your dollar or pound—meaning the price of most things has gone up. That's our old friend inflation. In most parts of the world, the rate of inflation in the past twenty or thirty years has been quite low, so the average price of things has gone up slowly—by around three percent a year. That means that something that cost one dollar last year would cost one dollar and three cents this year and one dollar and six cents next year. But even two or three percent each year gradually adds up. A dollar now would only buy half of what it would have bought twenty years ago.

20 YEARS LATER

Sometimes a currency starts losing its value really fast, and inflation runs out of control. This is called hyperinflation. It's happened in quite a few places, famously in Germany in the 1920s and most recently in Zimbabwe. The highest inflation rate ever recorded was in Hungary, just after World War II. In July 1946, prices in pengö, the currency in Hungary at the time, were doubling every fourteen hours or so, which meant that a loaf of bread cost ten times as much on Wednesday morning as it had on Monday morning. As soon as people got any pengö at all, they rushed out to spend them, before they lost all their value. Mostly people just stopped using them and bartered for things instead or used gold or foreign currency, like dollars. Of course this couldn't go on, and in August 1946, the Hungarian government introduced a new kind of currency called the forint, each of which was worth 400 octillion (that's 400,000,000,000,000,000,000,000,000,000) pengö. The old currency was essentially worthless; anyone who had any savings in it lost all their money, exactly as if a bank had collapsed.

It's not just the amount you can buy with a unit of currency that is always changing. The exchange rate—the amount a currency is worth in other currencies—changes, too.

Back in 1945, you could swap one British pound for four U.S. dollars, but by 2012, you would only get one and a half dollars for a pound. At the same time, the Japanese yen became much more valuable. In 1945, you could exchange one dollar for 360 yen, but by 2012, a dollar was worth just 80 yen.

There are lots of reasons exchange rates change. Inflation is one of them. The currencies of countries with high inflation rates usually lose value compared with those with low inflation rates. The interest rate is another. If banks in a country start to pay a lot of interest, the value of the currency of that country often goes up.

Governments try to control exchange rates but usually find that that's easier said than done. Something happens to mess up their plans and the value of their currency ends up changing, usually not as much and as quickly as in Hungary in the 1940s, but enough to make it obvious that money is a lot harder to control than they — and the rest of us — like to think it is.

— The price of everything and the value of nothing —

 **SO,** there you have it. Money has been around a long long time, but it's still strange slippery stuff, hard to pin down, always appearing and disappearing and existing only when people agree it exists. It might seem easy to count—that's one reason it's so useful—but no one can actually tell you how much of it there is around (although people who spend their time counting it might disagree about that).

In the end, can we say whether it's a good thing or a bad thing? Well, it was obviously a brilliant invention—it's helped people trade and carry out business in ways that simply wouldn't be possible without it. It's shaped the modern world as much as the invention of the plow, the wheel, or the steam engine. In fact it's almost impossible to imagine life these days without it. And that may be where part of the trouble lies.

We seem to have got into the habit of thinking about pretty much everything in terms of money. How much does it cost? How much is it worth? How much have I got to spend? Have I got more than you have? When you start thinking like that most of the time, there's a danger that you start believing that buying and selling are the only important things in life, and that anything that can't be bought and sold doesn't really count. And that also means it's easy to start believing that all you need in life is to have as much money as possible. I don't know what you think, but I don't think that is a particularly good thing.

— Author's Note —

I remember years ago asking someone who seemed to know a lot about the subject, "Where does all the money come from?" "The future," he replied. I was puzzled—didn't people dig it out of a hole in the ground or something? The question niggled away at me, so when my friend (and editor) Caz first mentioned the idea of writing about money—quite a while ago now—I jumped at the chance. We were both a bit surprised when other people thought it would be rather boring to read about. But then, in the fall of 2008, there was a big crisis and it looked as if most of the money in the world might disappear very quickly. How could that happen? What would happen next? How would we cope? Nobody seemed to know. It dawned on lots of people that perhaps they didn't understand money very well, and that it might be interesting to find out a bit more after all.

I certainly found it fascinating trying to get my head around it. I thought a lot, read a lot, thought a bit more, visited the money gallery in the British Museum in London to look at dolphin money from the Black Sea, ancient banknotes, and the first credit cards. I decided I understood money quite well. Then I decided I didn't really have a clue, but nor did anybody else. But as I went on, I began to see what the person I'd asked all those years ago was getting at. If you've read this far, and think you have some idea, too, then I figure I've done a pretty good job.

— Bibliography —

I read many articles and entries on the Internet while doing my research, some of which were useful and some of which weren't. Three books I learned a lot from were *Money: A History,* edited by Catherine Eagleton and Jonathan Williams (Buffalo, NY: Firefly, 2007); *Frozen Desire: The Meaning of Money* by James Buchan, (New York: Farrar, Straus and Giroux, 1997); and *The Ascent of Money: A Financial History of the World* by Niall Ferguson (New York: Penguin, 2008).

— Index —

Martin Jenkins is the author of several nonfiction books for young readers, including *Ape* and *Can We Save the Tiger?*, both illustrated by Vicky White. About *The History of Money*, he says, "Working on this book was fascinating: I thought a lot, read a lot, thought a bit more, and visited the money gallery in the British Museum in London to look at dolphin money from the Black Sea, ancient banknotes, and the first credit cards." Martin Jenkins lives in Cambridge, England.

Satoshi Kitamura is a past winner of the Mother Goose Award, given to the most exciting newcomer to British children's book illustration. About *The History of Money*, he says, "I enjoy the way this book explains how our lives are structured. The way the story is told gave me lots of ideas for cartooning—I wish the book was longer so that I could draw even more!" Satoshi Kitamura lives in Japan.